THE GREAT BAGEL & LOX BOOK

Photography by Battman

Distributed in the United States by Battman Studios
New York, New York

Published by Battman Studios
Text and Photographs © 2004 by Battman
All rights reserved. Printed in Hong Kong

ISBN 0-933477-14-7

www.battmanstudios.com

Book design by Lisa Sragg, En Moda Design, New York

Front cover photographed at Le Cirque, New York
Back cover photographed at The Four Seasons, New York

The Restaurants — The Chefs — Page

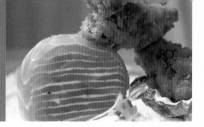

Forward

Look at these beautiful pictures and try not to salivate. This is not your typical New York brunch.

It's hard to believe that all of these dazzling creations, equally sculptural as they are gastronomic, all sprang from one deceptively simple challenge and two classic foods. "Take the bagel and lox and do something new." That was the request from Alan *BATTMAN* Batt, one of New York's premier photographers, to this city's most daring and celebrated chefs. To some, tampering with bagels and lox would verge on sacrilege. For many New Yorkers, bagels and lox is tantamount to a membership badge. But to these virtuosos of the kitchen and the camera, this was an invitation to use unfettered creativity and some good humor to display brilliance.

To understand how form is being manipulated or conventions broken, one must first understand the original. I think this is where Russ & Daughters steps in and why Alan Batt (or simply Battman to his friends) came to me with his meshuggenah (crazy) but wonderful project. For four generations, the Russ family has been hand-slicing perfectly smoked, cured and pickled fish, doling out schmears of cream cheese, serving up fresh bagels and bialys, as well as some free over-counter therapy and comedy to our customers thus preserving a food tradition that is an undeniable part of New York's cultural heritage. Bagels and lox is much more than the sum of its parts. For the people who line up outside our door on a weekend morning, the combination encapsulates childhood, family, tradition, and the old world. Bagels and lox have been there for all of life's rites of passage, births, mitzvahs, weddings and deaths. Now that's a versatile nosh.

In the beginning there was the word; and the word was *lox*. But *lox*, is not the catch-all term for smoked salmon that is used today. Genuine lox—originating from the German *lachs* for salmon—is not smoked at all; it is salt-cured salmon generally from the belly of the fish. Since earliest times, prior to refrigeration, foods were preserved in one of three ways; they were salted, marinated or smoked. In the mid to late 1800's the waters of both the Northern Atlantic and Northern Pacific coasts were teaming with salmon. The newly established railroad system in the late 1800's allowed for salmon to be transported cross country while preserved in large casks filled with salt. In the late 1880's the West Coast salmon supply was so ample that salmon were being transshipped to the old world. Some of the salmon remained in New York and satisfied the taste for salt-cured fish among the Eastern European immigrants, many of whom settled in the ghetto of the Lower East Side.

Customers at Russ & Daughters are occasionally dumfounded when they casually request a bagel and lox (sliced thin of course) and our countermen kindly explain that that is probably not what they really want. The saltiness of belly lox does not tend to appeal to modern tastebuds. They are probably looking for smoked salmon of which we carry eight different varieties. But for those who grew up on real belly lox or came directly from the mother country, there is only one lox. I don't know when exactly the term *lox* became to smoked salmon what Xerox is to copy machines, but linguistic evolution is a hard current to swim against. So here I too will indulge in perpetuating the misnomer by keeping the name *bagels and lox*. It just has that ring.

Smoked salmon, what most people mean when they say lox, appeared in the late 1920's. The first fish smoking was done by small independent smokers primarily from Germany, and the process is still very much the same. Salmon are placed in a wet cure of salt, brown sugar and water. With the advent of refrigeration, the salmon did not require such heavy salting. This mild cure was used for both Nova Scotia and West Coast salmon and is typically what we think of as *Nova Scotia* or *Nova* respectively. Wood chips—oak, hickory, apple or cherry depending upon the preference—are then burned and the smoke is wafted over the salmon for a period of about twelve hours. As the temperature never rises above approximately seventy-four degrees Fahrenheit, this is considered a *cold* smoking process.

As the concept of smoked salmon took hold, North Atlantic wild salmon became commercially fished out due to lack of conservation regulations. To replace the depleted salmon stock, the aquaculture industry, first begun in Norway, was born. Today, between ninety to ninety-five percent of salmon consumed around the world is farmed. The success of farmed salmon has allowed people all over the world to develop a taste for salmon; and while it has helped ward off extinction of the wild salmon population, recent warnings of the farming practices and effects on the wild population must be heeded as well.

And now what about the bagel? What makes this bread different from all other bread? This round bread with a hole is made very simply of high-gluten flour, salt, water, yeast and malt. The dough is first boiled before it is baked, and it is this two-part process that distinguishes it from other bread. The origins of the bagel are somewhat mythical and varied. One particularly colorful account is that in 1683 a Viennese baker baked a special bread to honor King John II Sobieski of

Poland, who had saved the city from Turkish invaders. As the king was a skilled horseman, the baker fashioned the bread in the shape of a *bügel*, or *stirrup* in German. Several hundred years later, the bagel made its way to America where they were prepared in basement bakeries and sold off of pushcarts probably alongside my grandfather. The bagel and lox may have coexisted, but they were not yet conjoined. Originally, bagels were to be eaten on their own much like a pretzel. They were thinner and smaller with a higher crust to dough ratio than the plumped up variations we see today. The first known accompaniment to the bagel in Europe was goose fat. Some say that cream cheese, which was first marketed by the Breakstone brothers in the 1920's, was introduced as a way to prevent foods from falling through the bagel's hole. Another story is that the cream cheese was used to cut the salty taste of the lox. Bagels became bigger and thicker to accommodate accompaniments to put on it. Bagels increased in mass appeal in the 1950's when Harry Lender, a Jewish baker from Lublin, Poland, worked towards his dream of seeing "a bagel in every toaster." Lender was able to introduce the bagel to the national market by eliminating the traditional hand-rolling and boiling process in favor of steaming and flash freezing. The commercialization of the bagel helped seal its place in the American food cannon, but it also resulted in such abomination as blueberry bagels, jalapeño bagels and even bagel pizza. Sadly enough, with most bagels today being machine-made, super-sized and loaded with sugar, even most New Yorkers today don't know from a *real* bagel. But what we as New Yorkers do have working in our favor is our water. This special ingredient is why the claim that it is hard to find a decent bagel outside of New York has yet to be debunked.

To this day no one knows when or how the bagel and lox first met. The earliest recollection of the Russ family selling the combination was in the 1940's. Before then, lox and nova were eaten on corned rye or black bread. Russ & Daughters only started selling bagels on Saturdays when the bakers were closed for Shabbat. I think my grandfather, Joel Russ, the founder of Russ & Daughters, would be shocked to know that people were trying to pinpoint the genesis of the bagel and lox with historical accuracy. He would have found it similarly unfathomable that the wares he sold off of his pushcart on Orchard Street would now be considered a New York delicacy and pictures of it would be sitting on someone's coffee table for pure aesthetic appeal. But the evolution of the bagel and lox from immigrant to glamorous status parallels the evolution of Russ & Daughters itself.

Joel Russ arrived on New York's Lower East Side at the turn of the century. He was a Galitzianer, a Jew whose homeland was historically flip-flopped between being Russian Poland and Polish Russia. Upon arriving in the immigrant ghetto, Joel quickly set up shop, or more precisely a pushcart, on Orchard Street, the neighborhood's commercial thoroughfare. In 1914, he graduated from a pushcart to a store. His first wares were salted lox and salted herring. These *appetizing* foods were separated from delicatessen since, according to Kosher law, fish and dairy could not be prepared or consumed with meat. Russ had no sons, and being an economizing entrepreneur, he pulled in his three young daughters, Hattie, Ida and Anne. From the age of twelve they learned the art of slicing salmon and did not shy away from plunging their tiny hands to the depths of the herring barrel. In my revisionist mind I'd like to think of my grandfather as a pioneering feminist who promoted women in the workplace. But in reality, Joel needed help and figured that his family might as well bear some of the tsores (the headaches and hardships). The three Russ daughters met their husbands in the store, and they too were summoned into the business. The irony is that my parents worked hard so that their children would know something different. That was, after all, the general sequence of events on the Lower East Side: do well enough so that you can leave. After practicing law for ten years, I actually chose the opposite route. As a recovering attorney, I have found happiness and meaning in selling bagels and lox.

Today, as the third-generation proprietor of our store, I find myself presiding over one of the last remaining appetizing shops in this city (in my grandfather's day there were twenty to thirty similar shops on the Lower East Side). But Russ & Daughters, like the iconic bagel and lox, is no monument to the past. It is still, ninety years later, vibrant with life brought by younger generations of followers. Moreover, the recent renaissance of the now bustling Lower East Side, has made neighborhood institutions like Russ & Daughters that much more embedded in its cultural landscape. In much the same way that Russ & Daughters has helped define the Lower East Side by holding on to its history and character, so too, by staying true to what we have always done—bagels and lox being one of them—have we allowed these fantastic chefs to celebrate the new. A bagel spoon dipped in salmon mousse? Kosher cannolis stuffed with smoked salmon and tofu cream cheese? Smoked salmon foie gras? It is all here in this splendid book for at least your eyes to feast on.

There is an amusing sign that hangs in Russ & Daughters. It reads, "Lox et Veritas," meaning Lox (as opposed to *lux* or light) and Truth. Having marveled at the photographic eye of Battman and the virtuoso creations of these esteemed chefs, another statement becomes evident, "Lox et Ars", Lox is indeed art.

Mark Federman— 3rd Generation Russ & Daughters

Atelier

Executive Chef | Gabriel Kreuther

Poppy seed bagel, gravlax, cream cheese, salmon roe,
red onion, chives, cucumber, red pearl onion, olive oil,
lemon juice, balsamic vinegar, chive oil, salt, pepper

Executive Chef | Andy D'Amico

Smoked salmon niçoise with panisse, chives,
quail eggs, chive cream cheese, tomatoes. olives

a n n i s a

Executive Chef | Anita Lo

Sockeye salmon belly sashimi, shiso leaf,
tea smoked and salted egg round,
yellow heirloom plum tomato,
black soy and sesame sauce, fresh wasabi,
to be served with a tempura bits

kitchen22

Chef de Cuisine | Scott Romano

Salmon gravlax, tom olives,
crisp salmon skin, salmon oil, micro greens

'wichcraft

Executive Chef | Sisha Ortuzar

Fresh white salmon belly with pickled mustard seeds,
bagel panzanella with plain and pumpernickel bagel croutons,
pickled red onion, heirloom tomato, cucumber, basil, capers,
extra virgin olive oil, red wine vinegar, sea salt, black pepper

BLUE HILL

Co-Chefs | Michael Anthony
Dan Barber

Citrus-cured salmon and bagel slice with herring roe,
pickled fennel, black olive purée,
fingerling potatoes, capers, preserved lime

Chef de Cuisine | Amanda Freitag

Smoked salmon, cream cheese, mascarpone, caper berries,
red and yellow tomatoes, red onion, fennel, ciabatta

Executive Chef | Nicholas Type

Hot Dog: Atlantic salmon, carrots, parsley, dill,
capers, onions, cream, spices, hot dog bun
Topping: créme fraîche and caviar
Garnish: lemon slice and parsley

meatball

beignets

fries

dips

Executive Chef | Sue Torres

Corn tortilla chip, mezcal cured salmon,
diced avocado & black bean sauce, lime segments,
chive points, chile de arbol garnish, frisée with lime vinaigrette
Sauces: smoked pepper coulis, yellow pepper coulis

Executive Chef | Michael Ginor

Sauternes cured gravlax,
terrine of Hudson Valley foie gras,
Maui onion marmalade

Atelier

Chef de Cuisine | Shaun Hergatt

Poppy seed bagel chips, lox, cream cheese, sour cream,
chives, red onion, olive oil, salt, pepper, mixed salad greens,
pink peppercorn oil, dill, Iranian osetra caviar

SUSHISAMBA
on park

Executive Chef | Nitzan Raz

Spicy yucca cracker, cachaça-cured salmon,
cream cheese espuma, yellow peppers, greens

Chango

Executive Chef | Joseph A. Cacace

Baked flour tortillas, tequila cured salmon,
chipotle créme fraîche, flying fish roe

FAUCHON
PARIS

Executive Chef │ Florian Bellanger

Norwegian salmon, créme fraîche,
Fauchon croissant,
sea salt, chives, cracked pepper

ALAIN DUCASSE
at the ESSEX HOUSE

Chef de Cuisine | Elena Didier

Smoked salmon, bagel, poppy seeds,
caviar, sour cream, romaine lettuce, onion

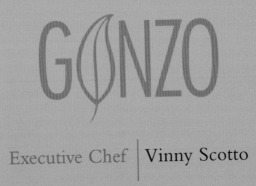

GONZO

Executive Chef | Vinny Scotto

Bruschetta with robiola, cured cheese & grappa,
smoked salmon, tomato, corn relish

restaurant

ROUGE

Chef | Sarah Beth Scherer

Bagel puffs, smoked salmon soufflé, eggs, caviar

MARCH
RESTAURANT

Executive Chef | Wayne Nish

"Few things in life are perfect as they are.
When you find one, cherish it. The Jewish delicatessen icon
that is Nova and cream cheese on a bagel with tomato and onion
is one of them. To add to it is to take away from it." *Wayne Nish*

Executive Chef | Jake Klein

Bagels, chive cheese, Dr. Brown's soda, red onion,
tomatoes, kippered salmon, Nova lox, lox wings,
gravlax, chives, egg yolks, capers

Executive Chef | Michael Lockard

Bagel tuile,
crystalized dill,
salmon ice cream

Fleur de Sel

Executive Chef | Cyril Renaud

Atlantic smoked salmon, fresh mango, chive créme fraîche, crêpe

Executive Chef | Denis Fitzgerald

Sesame seed, poppy, cinnamon & everything bagels,
smoked salmon mousse, ricotta cheese, purée of spinach, chives,
sun-dried tomatoes, marinated salmon, halibut, fresh tuna

heart*beat*

Executive Chef | John Mooney

Lox, pumpernickle bagel, petite joaquin,
caper berries, chervil, lemon

NORMA'S

Executive Chef | Emile Castillo

Bagel, smoked salmon, beluga caviar,
Boursin cheese, cucumbers, assorted veggies

LEVER HOUSE RESTAURANT BAR

Executive Chef | Dan Silverman

Bagel, gravlax, cream cheese, capers

Chef de Cuisine | Douglas Psaltis

Lox, caper & dill cream cheese, bagel chips,
red onion, tomato, capers, small salad & herbs

MONTRACHET

Executive Chef | Chris Geswaldi

Dill and cream cheese emulsion, bagel, créme fraîche,
green & red topico, smoked salmon,
osetra caviar, dill oil, Japanese seaweed salad

The Institute
of Culinary Education

Executive Chef | Andrew Gold

"Grilled New York Strip Salmon"
Grilled smoked salmon steak,
baked potato stuffed with chive cream cheese,
tomato & onion salad, assorted bagels

Executive Chef | David Pasternack

White salmon carpaccio

davidburke & donatella

Executive Chef | David Burke

Bagel chips, lox, créme fraîche, quail egg, caper berries

One if by Land,

Two if by Sea

Executive Chef | Gary Volkov

House smoked salmon with buckwheat blinis

Red Onion Soubise: red onion, rice, white wine, créme fraîche

Yellow Tomato Coulis: yellow tomatoes, shallot, bacon

inside

Executive Chef | Charleen Badman

Gravlax, salmon mousse,
cream cheese, bagels

JEAN GEORGES

Chef de Cuisine | Greg Brainin

Everything bagel, smoked salmon gelée, chive cream cheese

Executive Chef | Kirti Pant

Salmon fillet, naan, tandoori marinade, yogurt, red chili powder,
ginger garlic paste, salt, garam masala powder, lemon juice,
sour cream relish, sour cream, turmeric, ginger, green chili,
curry leaves, onion, mustard seeds, dill, chives

The River Café

Executive Chef | Brad Steelman

Fruitwood smoked salmon terrine,
crispy bagel crusted oysters

Executive Chef | Michael Lipp

Black sesame doughnut, mango créme bruleé,
coconut sorbet, sliced dried mango,
blackberries, strawberries, blueberries

THE FOUR SEASONS
R E S T A U R A N T

Executive Chef | Christian Albin
Chef de Cuisine | Fred Mero

Sliced Scottish smoked salmon, New York City bagels,
cream cheese with herbs, cream cheese with strawberries, cream cheese with roasted nuts

Executive Chef | Cheng-Hua Yang

Salmon, lettuce, bagel, carrots

FLATIRON

Executive Chef | Julie Reiner

Absolut citron, lemon juice, lime juice, horseradish,
Worcestershire sauce, celery salt, tobassco, black pepper,
pikkapeppa sauce, tomato juice
Swizel stick: bagel, lox, cream cheese, tomato

Ouest

Executive Chef | Tom Vallenti

Smoked salmon, cream cheese, bagel chips,
scallions, egg yolk, caviar

The Sea Grill

Executive Chef | Edward Brown

Sesame bagel chips, cream cheese, Nova belly lox,
scallions, beefsteak tomato, red Bermuda onion,
smoked sturgeon, salmon roe

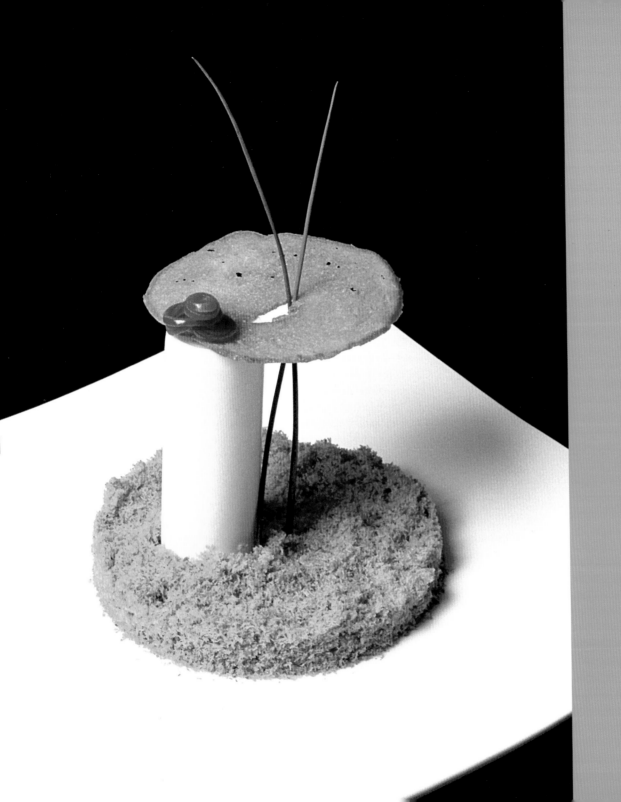

AUREOLE

Executive Chef | Dante Boccuzzi

Bagel crisp, smoked salmon dust, cream cheese tower,
verjus marinated red onion, chive points

Executive Chef | Claude Alain Solliard

Pumpernickel bagel, sun-dried tomato bagel, onion bagel,
cream cheese, chives, onions, lobster, smoked salmon,
watercress, Lasaviesanne kombu noodle, sugarcane

SUSHISAMBA
on seventh

Executive Chef | Michael Cressotti

The BLT: Wild king salmon, quesco blanco & edamame salsa, toasted sesame bagel, chive oil, crushed pink peppercorn

THE BILTMORE ROOM

Chef | Gary Robins

Tataki of smoked salmon, bialy crostini with créme fraîche & caviar,
cucumber ginger sorbet, fennel jicama salad

86

layla

Executive Chef | Carrie Starcher

Cream cheese, milk, capers, red onions, black pepper,
smoked salmon, bagels, chopped tomatoes
Garnish: Chopped herbs, capers, red onion

SOHOGRANDHOTEL

Chef de Cuisine | Missy Robbins

Bagel chips with salmon mascarpone mousse

Le Bernardin

Executive Chef | Eric Ripert

Bagel, lox, cream cheese, caviar

Executive Chef | Jay Shaffer

Smoked salmon custard, créme fraîche, beluga caviar,
bagel spoon with mustard seeds & salt

ida mae

Executive Chef | Kenneth Collins

Pumpernickel bagel, duck trap farm smoked salmon tower,
sweet potato cream cheese, red onion marmalade,
white figs, chive, chervil oil

good enough to eat

Executive Chef | Carrie Levin
Chef | James Brockman

Potato latke, lemon fresh yogurt, smoked salmon,
salmon roe, egg, red onion, chives

NOBU

Chef de Cuisine | Ricky Estrellado

Lox, bagel, wasabi, cream cheese,
mayo, micro greens, lemon zest, fresh red chili,
reduce balsamic vinegar, green onion

Executive Chef | Rick Moonen
Chef de Cuisine | Matthew Accarrino

Fennel cured wild salmon roulade

Wet marinade: red onion juice, fresh fennel juice, kosher salt,
sugar, fennel tops, toasted fennel seeds

Mandarin orange blossom cream: créme fraîche, Hanger One Mandarin
Blossom Vodka, fresh orange juice, gelatin, orange zest

Sweet onion relish: white onions, olive oil, jalapeño peppers,
red bell peppers, sugar, champagne vinegar

soHOGRANDHOTEL

Executive Chef | Gabriel Sorgi

Smoked and fresh salmon, fine herbs, créme fraîche

Executive Chef | Steven Duong

Filet of salmon, sticky rice, mung beans, vegetable oil,
roasted peanuts, cream cheese, turmeric, ginger, hot pepper,
garlic, fresh dill, lime juice, sugar, fish sauce, cucumber

John's of Bleecker Street

Executive Chef | Michael Frank

Smoked salmon, olives, onions, peppers,
John's secret sauce, whole milk mozzarella

Executive Chef | Michael Lomonaco

Wood fired flatbread, smoked salmon, roasted piquillo peppers,
goat cheese & herbs, manchego cheese, chorizo sausage,
greens, extra virgin olive oil

Tribeca Grill

Executive Chef | Stephen Lewandowski

House smoked salmon, potato latkas,
fennel compote, sunny side quail eggs

Food Stylist | Megan Fawn Schlow
Proprietor | Mark Federman

Grandma's potato soup recipe with lox and bagel croutons

MORRELLS

Executive Chef | Patricia Williams

Plain bagel, watercress, smoked salmon,
tomato, red onion, micro greens

OSTERIA DEL

CIRCO

Executive Chef | Albert Di Meglio

Smoked salmon, bagel, sun-dried tomatoes, goat cheese

AQUAVIT

Executive Chef | Marcus Samuelsson

Bagels, smoked salmon, cream cheese, old chef's jacket

The French Culinary Institute

NEW YORK CITY

Executive Chef | Dominic Cerrone
Chef | Susan Lifrieri

Bagel, pumpernickel bagel, rolled salmon, cream cheese, radishes,
cucumbers, capers, tomatoes, dill, poppy seeds, sesame seeds

Executive Chef | Pierre Schaedelin

Bagel, gravlax, quenelles of pike, caviar,
crustacean sauce, cream cheese, eggs

BLUE SMOKE

Executive Chef | Kenny Callaghan
Pastry Chef | Jennifer Giblin

Smoked salmon, fried bread, cream cheese

Executive Chef | Jacques Torres

Bagel: dark and vanilla modeling chocolate
Cream cheese: white chocolate ganache
Lox: strawberry fruit leather

BEPPE

Executive Chef | Cesare Casella

Pizza dough: Flour, water, extra virgin olive oil, yeast, salt, pepper

Everything mix: Poppy seeds, sesame seeds, caraway seed, garlic, onion

Toppings: Cured salmon, fresh mozzarella, greenmarket tomatoes, basil

Executive Chef | Brian Wieler
Sous Chef | Marissa Morgan

Smoked salmon, pancetta and Brie club sandwich

GRILL

| Executive Chef | Bobby Flay |
| Sous Chef | Christine Sanches |

Bagel, house cured salmon, cream cheese

LANDMARC

Chef | Frank Proto

Everything taralli, lox, mascarpone cheese

SHALLOTS

Executive Chef | Damian P. Sansonetti

Cannoli shaped bagel, smoked salmon, tofu cream cheese

Siam Inn

Executive Chef | Tanaporn Tangwibulchai

Lox, bagel, cream cheese, fried quail egg, sticky rice

Chef | Larry Kolar

Smoked salmon, frisée, roasted red peppers,
créme fraîche, crepé tied with chive

RIVE
GAUCHE

Executive Chef | Jerome Vidy

Smoked salmon, bagel, red onion, cucumbers,
red bell peppers, cream cheese, tomato, basil

Executive Chef | Erik Blauberg

Baby frisée, baby arugula, red onion, roma tomato concassé, smoked
salmon, chives, lemon juice, bagel chips, goat cheese
Garnish: chives, capers, paprika, goat cheese sauce
Goat Cheese Dressing: goat cheese, heavy cream, horseradish

Executive Chef | Ari H. Nieminen

Lox, toasted bagel, cucumber, cream cheese, dill,
Ms. Jaeme Griffen

The Chefs